Celtic Harp Music
of Carolan and others for
Solo Guitar

by Glenn Weiser

Thanks to Michael Carey, Scott Chinery and the Chinery Collection for
the use of the cover photo of the Larson Brothers Harp Guitar

ISBN 978-0-931759-95-6

Typesetting - Patricia Pomellitto
Cover Art - Kevin Delaney
Paste-up - Cindy Middlebrook

CENTERSTREAM Publications

P.O. Box 17878 Anaheim Hills, CA 92807
Phone/Fax (714) 779-9390 - E-Mail, Centerstrm @ AOL.com

This book is dedicated to my mother, Gladys Lawrence, who was born in Lisburn, Co. Antrim, on the soil of the land whose symbol is the harp.

I would like to thank Patricia Pomellitto for typesetting and designing this book ~ truly a labor of love.

Special thanks also go to John Roberts.

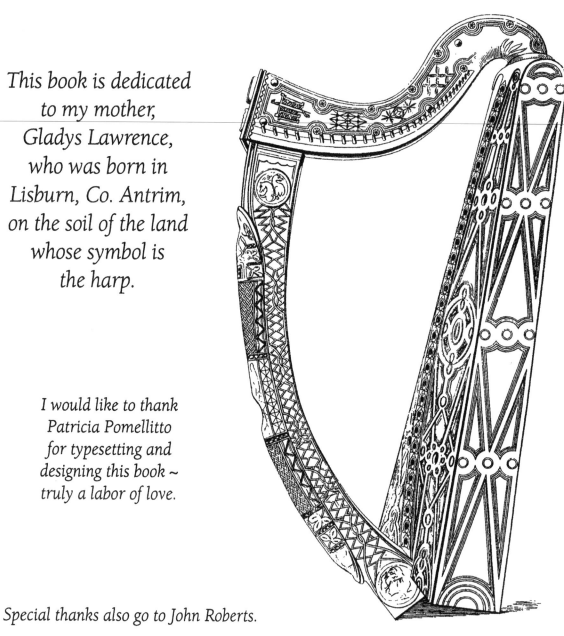

The Brian Boru Harp

Correspondence may be addressed to me at
Box 2551, Albany, N.Y. 12220

CELTIC HARP MUSIC OF CAROLAN
& OTHERS FOR SOLO GUITAR

ARRANGED BY GLENN WEISER

ABOUT THE AUTHOR

Glenn Weiser was born in Ridgewood, New Jersey in 1952 and began playing guitar at age 14. He studied classical guitar with Paul Battat and later ragtime fingerpicking with Eric Schoenberg. From there he went on to learn banjo, mandolin and harmonica. Glenn is the author of *Fiddle Tunes for Harmonica, Blues and Rock Harmonica,* (Centerstream Publishing) *and The Minstrel Boy (Celtic Guitar Arrangements).* He has also written for *Sing Out!* magazine and *Acoustic Guitar.* Glenn currently teaches and performs in the Albany, New York area.

INTRODUCTION

The oldest surviving harp in Ireland is known as the Brian Boru harp. According to legend it once belonged to the great 11th century Irish king who united the four provinces of Ireland against the Danes. This harp, from which the national symbol of Ireland is taken, is at Trinity College in Dublin and probably dates from the fourteenth century.

In 1961, after centuries of silence, it was re-strung with metal strings and played in the traditional manner by a harper with long, crooked nails. The tone was described as "bell-like with an added richness akin to that of a guitar."

Perhaps this is the reason why Celtic harp music sounds so beautiful on the guitar. Arrangements of harp tunes have been recorded by a number of finger-style and classical guitarists, including Piérre Bensusan, Eric Schoenberg, Narcisso Yepes, John Renbourn, and others.

This book contains forty-five Irish and Scottish harp tunes arranged for solo guitar. Twenty eight are by Turlough O'Carolan (see biographical notes), whose music has been undergoing a revival since the Irish band *The Chieftans* began recording it in the seventies. The remaining seventeen are all older tunes. Most of these are by known composers, but a few are anonymous.

The transcriptions here are mostly intermediate in terms of the difficulty. Standard tunings have been used throughout so that the book might appeal to the classical guitarist as well as the steel-string fingerstylist.

In working out the bass lines and inner voices of these pieces, I have usually followed the rules of harmony and counterpoint. Since Irish harp music was first notated in the late eighteenth century there has been a contrétemps over whether or not this kind of music can be successfully harmonized according to the old classical rules. In general, I think it can, as long as the settings are not too elaborate, and are diatonic (the only accidental I usually allow in the arrangements is the augmented fourth, which is most often used as the third of the V of V chord).

In these arrangements I have tried to come as close to the spirit, if not the actual sound of Celtic harp music, as possible. These tunes are some of the most beautiful music I know. It therefore gives me great joy to make this book available to guitarists and lovers of Celtic music.

~ G.W.

ABOUT THE CELTIC HARP

The harp was widely played in Ireland, Scotland, Wales and the Celtic parts of the Continent from at least the ninth century (the harp is depicted in an Irish stone carving from that period) until the seventeenth century. It was the principal instrument of the Celtic aristocracy and was also loved by the common people as well. The twelfth century monk-historian Geraldus Cambrensis remarked on the great skill of the Irish harpers, and their music was admired throughout Europe. This was attested to by another twelfth century writer, John of Salisbury, who wrote that "had it not been for the Irish harp, there would have been no music at all on the Crusades."

The harpers of Scotland evidently equalled their Irish counterparts in prowess ~ Cambrensis wrote that some even considered the Scots better players. Irish and Scottish harpers commonly visited each other's countries to study, learn, and exchange tunes. Four of the tunes in this book, for example, were composed by Irish harpers living in Scotland and some harp tunes have both Irish and Scottish names.

The harp was sturdily built of willow or other hardwoods and often elaborately decorated. The earlier ones had about a dozen or less strings, and the later ones about 35 to 43. In Ireland, harps had metal strings; Scottish ones were strung with gut. The sound chamber of the instrument was made by hollowing out a single piece of wood, and often served as a suitcase for a harpers' clothes when he was travelling (it was played by men only until the fifteenth century). Some professional harpers were regularly employed at the castles of Celtic chieftains, and others made their livings as itinerants by entertaining in the homes of the wealthy in exchange for their hospitality. Harpers were hired for weddings, funerals, Masses and other occasions.

The harpers' repertory consisted of songs and instrumental pieces. The lyrics to the Irish and Scottish songs were, as far as I know, in Gaelic (although this might not have been the case for Lowland harp tunes) and were often composed for the harpers' patrons.

The tragic extinction of the harping tradition at the beginning of the nineteenth century was caused by the Angloization of the Irish and Scottish cultures, the increased popularity of stepdancing and the fiddle, and the inability of the harp to play the accidentals required for classical music, which started coming into vogue in Dublin and Edinburgh during the Baroque era.

Because harp music had always been handed down orally, very little of it has been preserved. The most important attempt was made in 1792, when a gathering of harpers was convened in Belfast to compete for cash prizes. Only ten harpers, ranging in age from fifteen to over one hundred, could be found. A nineteen year old church organist named Edward Bunting was hired to notate the music, but with few exceptions only the melodies, and not the bass lines were taken down. This proved to be a historic oversight; now we know little about how the harp was actually played. However, judging from the few hundred melodies we do have, it is clear that harping was a high art. Some of the tunes are slow airs of great beauty while others are spirited dance tunes or robust marches. The lyrics of the songs, where known, have not been given here, but many of the tunes have interesting tales attached to them which are recounted in the accompanying notes.

In the late nineteenth century, interest in the Celtic harp was rekindled, but the tradition had been broken in all the Celtic countries except Wales. My grandmother played the harp in Northern Ireland, but when my grandfather took his family and emigrated to America, the harp had to be left behind.

In the last few decades the harp has grown in popularity. Harpers Derek Bell, Anne Heyman, Alison Kinnaird, Patrick Ball, and others have made wonderful records of Celtic music, (see Discography) and harp is often heard on "New Age" recordings. Harps are again being built by talented artisans and new players are performing and recording.

At one point during the Belfast gathering the harper Arthur O'Neill spoke of the impending demise of harping in Ireland to the young Edward Bunting. With a tear in his eye he exclaimed, "The dear sweet tunes! The dear sweet tunes!" Perhaps if O'Neill were alive today, he would smile instead.

~ G.W.

Turlough O'Carolan

ABOUT TURLOUGH O'CAROLAN

Turlough O'Carolan (1670 - 1738), the last of the great Irish harper-composers, was born near Nobber in County Meath. His father, John Carolan, was most likely a small farmer. He moved the family to the Roscommon-Lietrim district when Turlough was fourteen and eventually came to work for the MacDermott Roe family of Aldersford, who operated an iron foundry. Seeing promise in the boy, Mrs. MacDermott Roe provided him with an education until he was eighteen.

Then disaster struck and Turlough was blinded by smallpox. It was decided to make a harper of him so that he might have a means of livelihood, and he was given lessons on the harp for three years. After becoming proficient on his instrument, he was given a horse, a guide, and some money, and was sent out on the road as an itinerant harper.

But this was not a life of great hardship, as harpers were usually welcome to stay at the homes of the well to do and enjoy their hospitality in exchange for entertainment, and more importantly, the honor of having songs composed for and named after them by the bards.

This, then, was Carolan's modus vivendi ~ travelling, composing, and being the honored guest of men and women of distinction. That he travelled widely and extensively we know from the names of the patrons which appear as titles to his many tunes. These songs are often called "planxties" ~ the term planxty means roughly "composed in honor of" and was evidently coined by Carolan himself.

It was during Carolan's lifetime that Italian Baroque music started to become fashionable in the great houses of the Irish gentry. Bach was to remain largely unknown outside of Germany for about a century, and Handel's star was still rising in England. So Vivaldi, Corelli, and Geminiani were the gods of music to the cultured. Carolan heard this music, so far beyond the folk melodies of Ireland, and was deeply impressed. As a result, he ceased to be a traditional Irish harper, and became a classically influenced folk composer. In many of his tunes, Carolan tried to imitate the Italian style. But to do this fully was impossible for him for two reasons: firstly, he was blind and could not study the rules of harmony, counterpoint, and form, and secondly, his diatonic harp could not play all the accidentals required for classical music.

Despite the fact that Carolan lacked the means of becoming a Baroque composer, he nonetheless produced much wonderful music. The pieces (some 214 have survived) are a blend of folk and classical elements. Like most Irish folk tunes they usually have two parts - this is known as the binary form. In his tunes, there are often unusual melodic twists and turns, especially the second parts, which is how he tried to approximate the effect of Baroque thematic development. Not all his efforts were successful, but he did compose scores of lovely tunes.

Carolan lived to see his genius recognized, and when he died at age 68, he was a famous man in Ireland. Although the harping tradition died out within a century of his death, his tunes were handed down by fiddlers, pipers, and whistle players, and so lived on. We know that they hold a place of high esteem in Irish music by the presence of 75 of them in "O'Neill's Music of Ireland," the chief collection of Irish instrumental music. Almost every major Irish traditional band has recorded his music, and his tunes are of course prominent in the repertories of Celtic harpers. Even Beethoven arranged three of his tunes for piano. By transcribing this music for guitar, it is hoped that Carolan's music and that of the earlier harpers will continue to find new admirers among guitarists and audiences alike.

~ G.W.

Carolan's Compositions

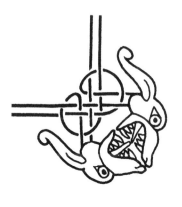

Lady Athenry

Turlough O'Carolan

This is generally considered to be one of Carolan's finest airs. George Petrie, the nineteenth century collector of Irish music, wrote of the air that, "It exhibits a greater gravity of character, and approaches more closely to the sober dignity of Corelli's gigas than perhaps any other compositions in the same class."

Arr. G. Weiser

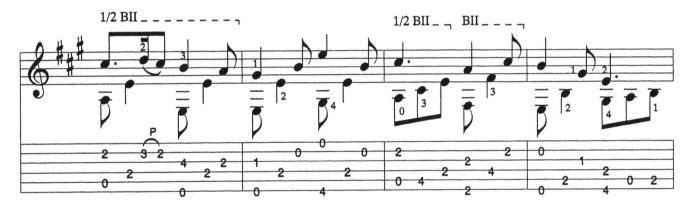

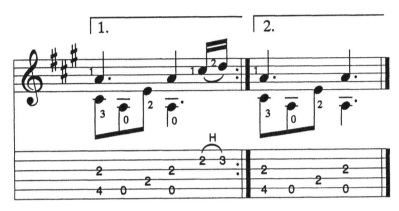

13

George Brabazon
2nd Air

There is some dispute as to whether this is a composition of Carolan's or a Scottish tune. It can be found in "O'Neill's Music of Ireland" under the title given above and also in the Scottish "Skye Collection" under the title "Prince Charlie's Welcome to the Isle of Skye." Carolan did precede Bonny Prince Charlie, though.

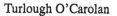

Turlough O'Carolan

Arr. G. Weiser

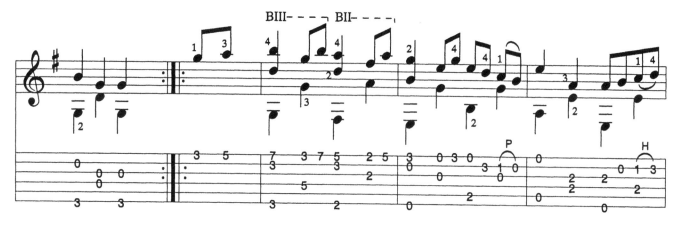

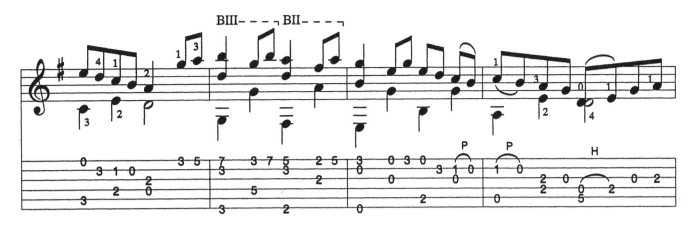

*Alternate Harmony, A part, fifth measure

Brighid Cruis
3rd Air

Brighid Cruis was a woman whom Carolan was enamored of from his youth. It is said that Carolan once recognized her form the touch of her hand, after not having met her for many years. These two airs are to be played as a medley.

Turlough O'Carolan

Arr. G. Weiser

4th Air

19

Dr. John Hart,
Bishop of Achonry

This air, according to Charles O'Conor, an Irish scholar who knew Carolan and was the subject of one of Carolan's tunes, "has often excited sentiments of the most fervent piety." Dr. Hart was a Catholic clergyman who was dispossessed of his land by an act of deceit. He was known for his kindness to birds, particularly caged birds, which he released whenever possible. According to a legend, when he died, all the birds in the locality assembled at his funeral and chanted his requiem.

Turlough O'Carolan

Arr. G. Weiser

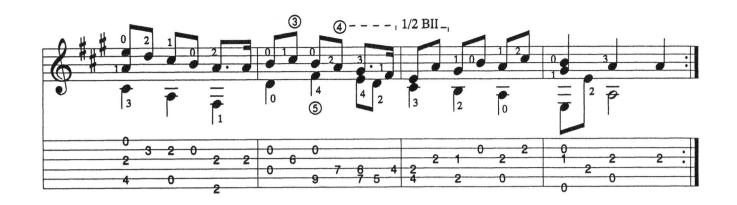

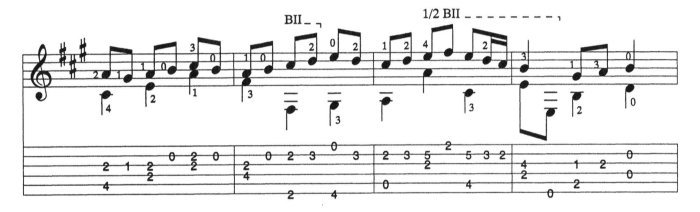

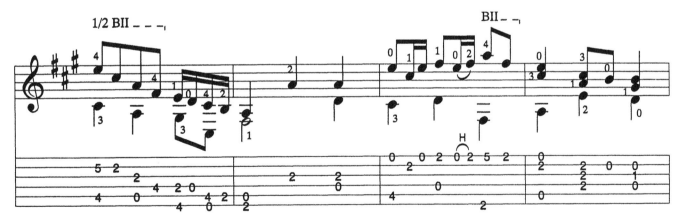

21

Planxty Hewlett

A lively drinking song. The subject remains unidentified.

Turlough O'Carolan

Arr. G. Weiser

* Alternate Harmony: B part, Measures 8-10

23

Lord Inchinquin

This beautiful tune has been recorded by the Chieftains. It was written for the fifth Earl of Inchinquin.

Turlough O'Carolan

Arr. G. Weiser

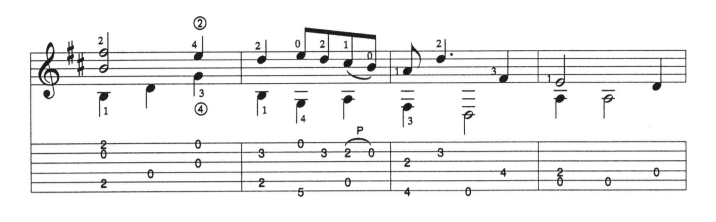

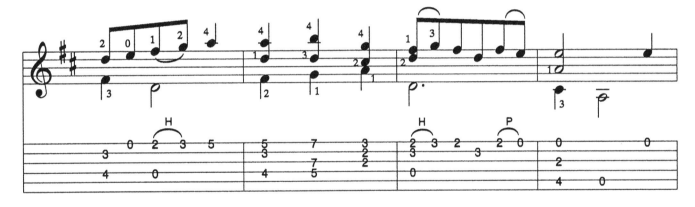

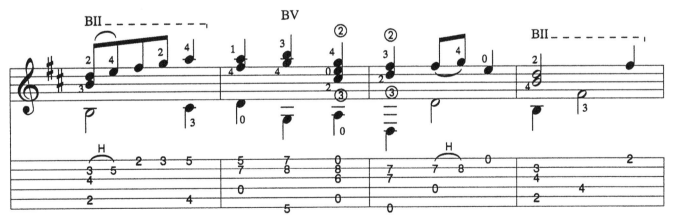

25

Col. John Irwin

This version is slowed down somewhat from the allegretto tempo marking given by Donal O'Sullivan, who wrote Carolan's biography and collected his tunes (see Bibliography). It strikes me as being the quintessential fond farewell.

Turlough O'Carolan

Arr. G. Weiser

Madam Judge

This air was composed for Abigail Judge, wife of Thomas Judge of Grangebey, County Westmeath, whom she married in 1707, and can be found in the Bunting Collection. It has been recorded by the Chieftains on their ninth album in a version that is similar to Bunting's arrangement, with the exception of the naturalization of the C sharp that occurs in the seventh measure of the second part. In light of the Celtic harp's limited chromatic capabilities, I have followed Derek Bell's lead in playing this note as a C natural. It's worth mentioning that another version of this tune was arranged for piano by Beethoven for the music publisher George Thompson of Edinburgh (Opus 108 ~ Scottish and Irish songs).

Turlough O'Carolan

Arr. G. Weiser

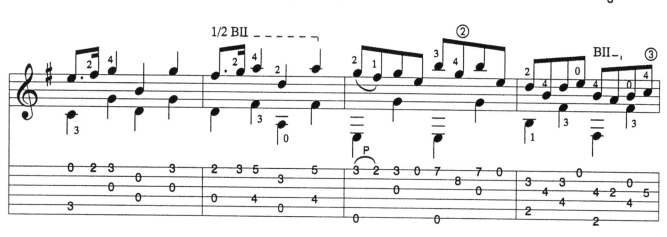

Mabel Kelly

This one is unusual as it starts on the subdominant chord (G in the key of D) and ends on the dominant (A) chord rather than the usual tonic. Derek Bell has this on his first album of Carolan tunes.

Turlough O'Carolan

Arr. G. Weiser

Elizabeth MacDermott Roe

This air is one of Carolan's most tender melodies and amply demonstrates the depth of feeling
Carolan must have had for the family that showed him so much kindness when he was young.
Elizabeth was the daughter and Henry and Anne were the parents.

Turlough O'Carolan

Arr. G. Weiser

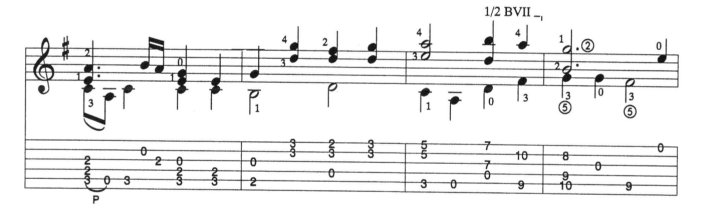

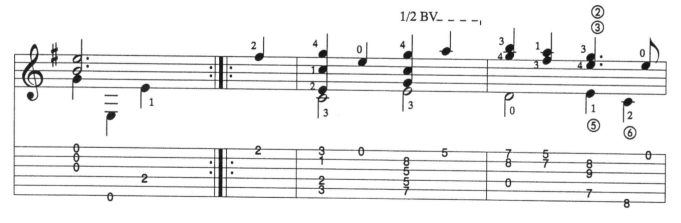

Morgan Magan

Turlough O'Carolan

This is one of Carolan's better known tunes and has been recorded by the Chieftains. This is their version, which is somewhat different from the variation found in O'Sullivan's book.

Arr. G. Weiser

Mrs. Maxwell

1st Air

This an be heard on Derek Bell's first solo album. A lively, graceful tune.

Turlough O'Carolan

Arr. G. Weiser

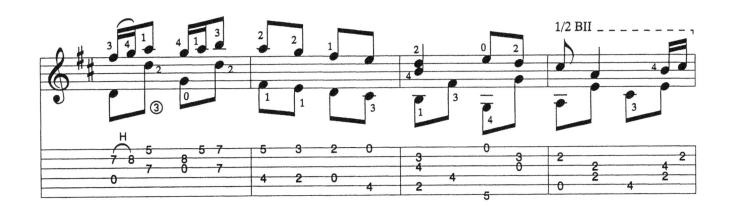

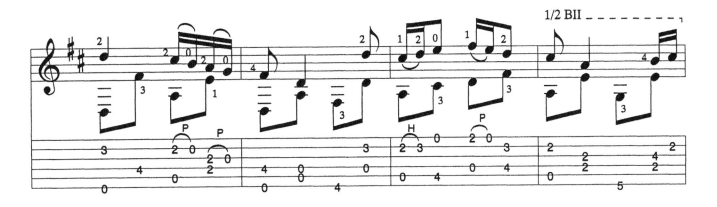

John O'Connor

There is an amusing anecdote in the harper Arthur O'Neill's Memoirs about this tune. For a gallon of whiskey promised in a bet, a harper named Thady Eliot played this tune during mass on Christmas Day at the time of the Elevation instead of the usual church music. The priest, who couldn't speak during this portion of the mass, stamped his feet in protest, causing the congregation to exclaim, "Heavens, the priest is dancing!" Thady got the whiskey but lost his job in the church.

Turlough O'Carolan

Arr. G. Weiser

Michael O'Connor
(jig from 1st air)

Donal O'Sullivan calls this jig "an unusually good one." The identity of the subject is uncertain.

Turlough O'Carolan

Arr. G. Weiser

* Alternate fingering: B part, third and fourth measures

Hugh O'Donnell

This fine jig can be heard on Derek Bell's second album of Carolan's airs.

Turlough O'Carolan

Arr. G. Weiser

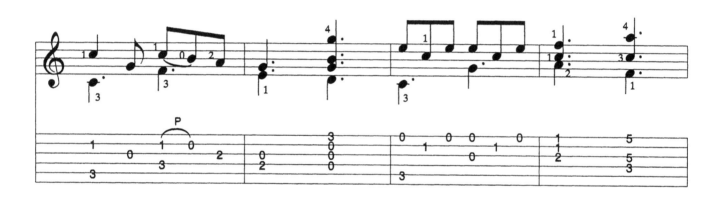

Planxty O'Flinn

This is considered one of Carolan's best. O'Sullivan guesses that it was probably composed for the butler at the MacDermott Roe house at Alderford who brought Carolan his last drink.

Turlough O'Carolan

Arr. G. Weiser

Katherine O'More

Turlough O'Carolan

This is Carolan's reworking of "Port Atholl". This setting can be heard on Derek Bell's second solo album.

Arr. G. Weiser

Fanny Poer

This piece, like "Colonel John Irwin," has been slowed down here.

Turlough O'Carolan

Arr. G. Weiser

⑥ = D

Mrs. Poer
(Carolan's Concerto)

Turlough O'Carolan

This is one of Carolan's most famous tunes and is considered to be one of the compositions where the Italian Baroque influence is particularly evident.

Arr. G. Weiser

Lady St. John

Turlough O'Carolan

This can be heard on Derek Bell's second Carolan album. Note the calls and responses in between the treble and bass in the second part. This is easy for the harp but difficult for the guitar because of the guitar's more narrow range.

Arr. G. Weiser

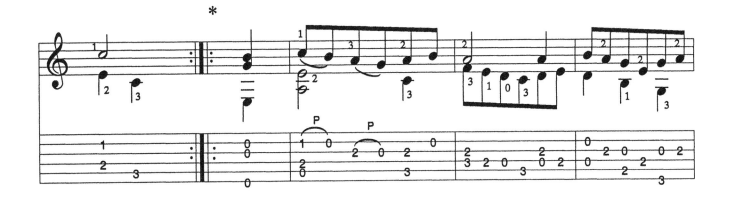

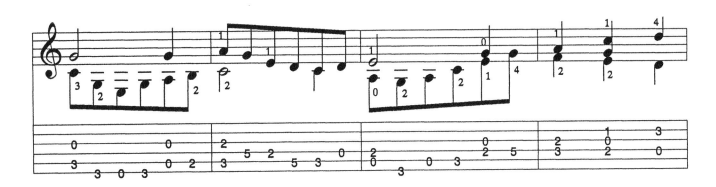

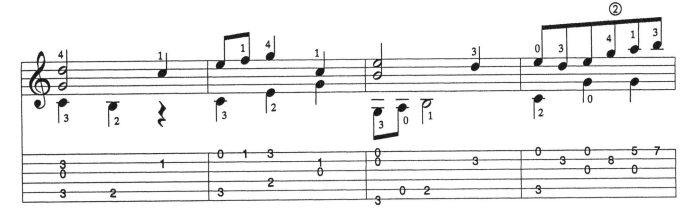

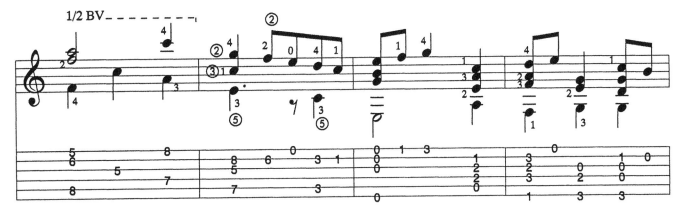

* Alternate Harmony: B part, measure 1

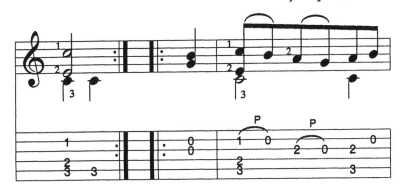

55

Dr. John Stafford
(Carolan's Receipt)

The legend goes that on one occasion Carolan felt unwell and went to see a doctor, who advised him to quit drinking. Carolan did this, but soon began feeling worse. Deciding that a second opinion was in order, he then turned to an old friend, Dr. John Stafford. Stafford told him that if Carolan would just play his harp, Stafford would give him a receipt ~ an archaic term for a prescription ~ for some whiskey. Carolan readily agreed to this. The two sat up drinking. Carolan played until his harp strings started breaking, and this wonderful tune was born.

Years later, Stafford attended on Carolan during his last illness and was one of the pallbearers at his funeral.

This arrangement was published in issue 3 of Acoustic Guitar (Nov-Dec '90).

Turlough O'Carolan

Arr. G. Weiser

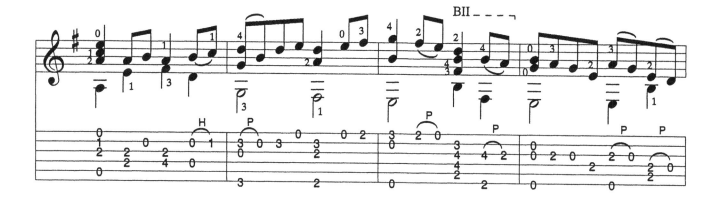

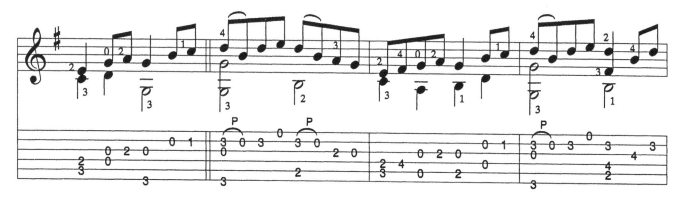

© 1995 CENTERSTREAM Publishing

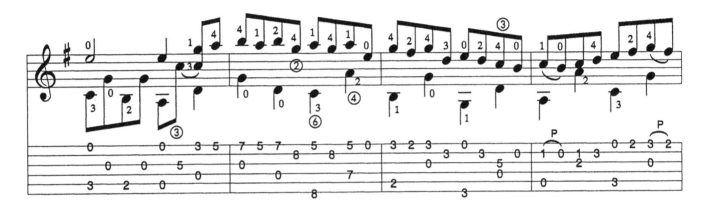

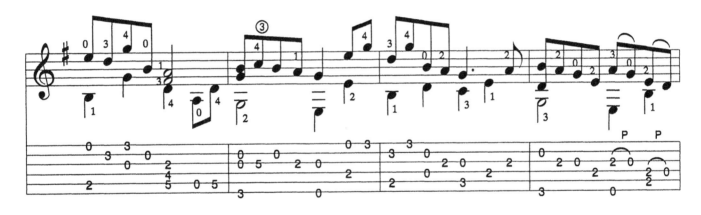

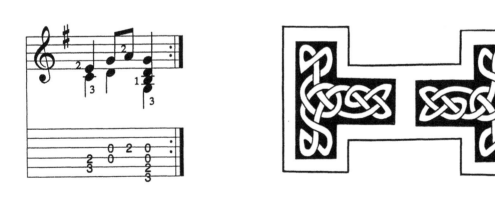

Carolan's Welcome
(No. 171)

Derek Bell calls it "Carolan's Welcome," but I don't know where he got the title. Anyway, it's a beautiful minor key tune.

Turlough O'Carolan

Arr. G. Weiser

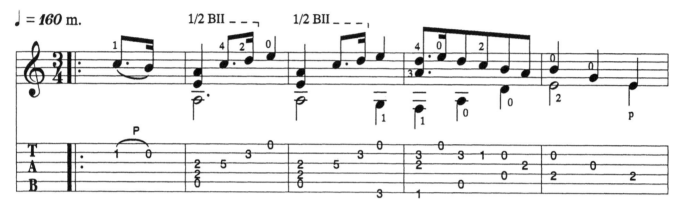

Planxty Browne
(No. 180)

"O'Neill's Music of Ireland" is the sole source of this jolly tune whose title O'Sullivan has dismissed as being unverifiable. The second part is particularly good.

Turlough O'Carolan

Arr. G. Weiser

Carolan's Farewell to Music

When Carolan was 68, he knew that the end was near. He decided to return to the MacDermott Roe home at Alderford and, upon arrival, called for the harp, played this haunting air, and was then led upstairs to what was to be his death-bed. This is considered to have been composed in the ancient Celtic style rather than the "Irish Baroque" of many of his famous tunes.

Turlough O'Carolan

Arr. G. Weiser

* Alternate Harmony: A part, measure 2.

Carolan's Quarrel with the Landlady

This is Carolan's version of an older tune called "Sit Down Under My Protection." Notice the interplay between the treble and the bass, representing the two arguing parties. This arrangement is based on Derek Bell's setting, which is slightly different from the one in O'Sullivan's book. An alternate harmony for the passage requiring a barre chord on the third fret, first appearing in the second measure, is given at the bottom of the page.

Turlough O'Carolan

Arr. G. Weiser

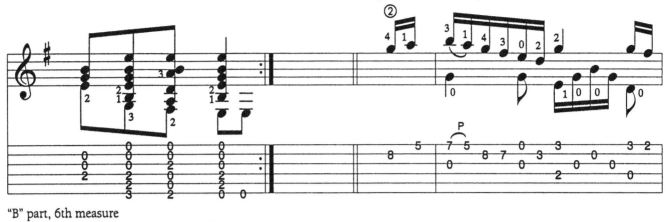

"B" part, 6th measure

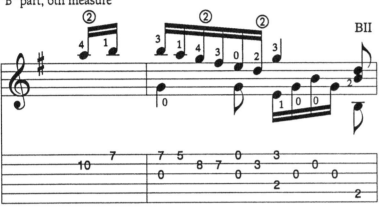

Sheebeg and Sheemore

Turlough O'Carolan

After Carolan left the MacDermott Roe house at age 21, his first stop was the home of a Squire Reynolds. Carolan played some tunes for his host, who was evidently unimpressed with the fledgling harper's ability. The squire asked him if he had done any composing. Carolan said he hadn't. Reynolds then told Carolan that he "might make a better hand of his tongue than his fingers," meaning that he might do better at composing than performing. He was going away for a few days, he added, and suggested a subject for a possible song, the nearby hills of Sheebeg (Little Hill) and Sheemore (Big Hill). According to legend two fairy armies had once fought a battle in between these hills. Perhaps Carolan could compose something on this theme by the time he got back.

Squire Reynolds returned a few days later to find Carolan playing "Sheebeg and Sheemore." Carolan's career as a composer had been launched.

⑥ = D

Arr. G. Weiser

♩ = *132* m.

Squire Wood's Lamentation
On Refusal of Ye Halfpence

In 1722, the English government authorized William Wood, a large mineowner and iron merchant, to mint an excessive amount of copper coinage for Ireland ~ much too much for the country's needs. The Irish were universally opposed to it and a successful boycott was organized, led by the merchants of Dublin. Carolan wrote lyrics to the tune, which was ascribed to him by George Petrie, the nineteenth century Irish tune collector. It turns out, though, that Carolan's melody is based on the Scottish tune "Soor Plooms" (sour plums), which was composed by the piper to the Laird of Galasheils around 1700. Scottish tunes were also adapted by Carolan for "Katherine O'More", "The Two William Davises", "Carolan's Cap", and possibly "George Brabazon" (second air).

Turlough O'Carolan

Arr. G. Weiser

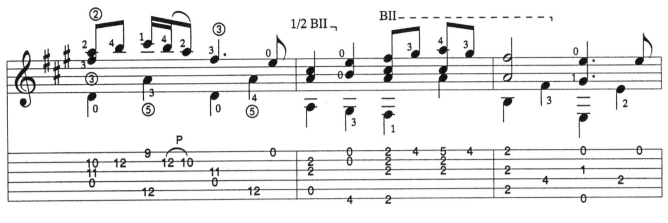

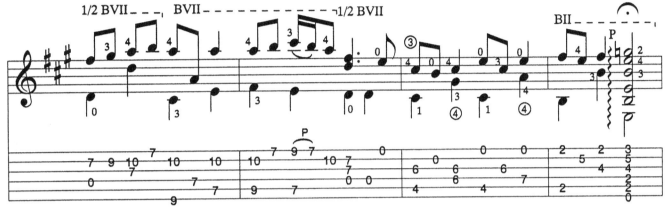

*Alternate Harmony, Measures 1-3, First Part

Irish & Scottish Harp Tunes

Brian Boru's March

Brian Boru was the famous Irish king who briefly united all Ireland before being killed fighting the Danes at the battle of Clontarf in 1014. This tune is undoubtedly very old and was the second piece that harp students had to learn during the Bardic Age.

Anonymous

Arr. G. Weiser

The Coolin

This is a very old tune that may date back as far as the thirteenth century, when the English passed laws forbidding young Englishmen from wearing the Irish hairstyle known as the coolin ~ something close to the "rat-tail" of the 1980's. In the lyrics to the tune, a young Irishwoman is enjoining other Irish maidens to marry the wearers of the coolin. The version given here was taken down from the singing of Patricia Cahill, a former nun who left the cloister on the advice of her mother superior to pursue a musical career.

Anonymous

Arr. G. Weiser

Eileen Aroon

Carol O'Daly

This famous Irish love song is the oldest Irish air to which lyrics are known to exist. It can be found in many different variants, which usually indicates that a tune is very old. The setting given here is from Edward Bunting's manuscript version of the air as played by Denis Hempson, who was the oldest harper that Bunting collected tunes from. Hempson's setting is longer than most other versions and the music fits the oldest known set of words to the song. Following the setting itself is a variation on the tune composed by the harper Cornelius Lyons, who was a contemporary of Turlough O'Carolan. In the manuscript version of the variation, measure five consists of a thirty-second note arpeggio pattern that requires great speed to play. There are two alternate versions of this measure following the piece: the first is the simplification that Bunting used in the printed version of the tune; the second is my own. Unless you're an advanced classical guitarist, you're probably better off with one of the alternate versions.

"Eileen Aroon" is ascribed to an Irish harper named Carol O'Daly, whom scholars place in either the thirteenth or seventeenth century. Because the O'Daly's were a family that produced poets for centuries, there is uncertainty as to which Carol O'Daly authored the song. According to the legend attached to the seventeenth century O'Daly, he was in love with Eileen Kavanaugh, who was the daughter of a nobleman. She was about to be wed to another man when O'Daly appeared in disguise at the ceremony and sang this song. Penetrating his disguise, the fair Eileen then eloped with the harper. But because the lyrics refer to the "spending of a cow," many scholars ascribe the tune to the thirteenth century O'Daly, as livestock was a medium of exchange in Ireland until about 1450.

In any event, the beauty of this song is such that when it was played for George Frederick Handel in Dublin in 1742, he exclaimed that he would rather have been the author of it than all his operas and oratorios(!).

Variation by Cornelius Lyons

Arr. G. Weiser

77

Bunting's published version: variation, measure 5

Simpler Yet (mine ~ GW)

Give Me Your Hand

Rory O'Cahan

This tune was composed in the seventeenth century by a blind Irish harper named Rory Dhall O'Caithan who spent many years in Scotland. According to the account of Arthur O'Neill, O'Caithan, who was of noble blood, visited the castle of a Lady Eglington, who, taking him for a commoner, demanded a tune in an abrupt manner. O'Caithan was offended by this unwitting breach of protocol and angrily left the castle. When Lady Eglington was informed of his rank, she arranged a reconciliation. O'Caithan returned to a more appropriate reception and composed the lovely tune "Give Me Your Hand" as a musical olive branch.

The tune subsequently spread all over Scotland, and O'Caithan was summoned to the court of the Scottish king James VI, who later as James I ascended to the English throne. The harper played the tune for the king, who then arose from the throne, walked over to O'Caithan and laid his hand on Rory's shoulder in a gesture of opprobation. "A greater hand than thine has laid upon my shoulder," said O'Caithan. "Who is that, man?" cried the king. "The O'Neill, my liege," O'Caithan boldly replied, referring to the king of Ulster. This version of this tune is from Bunting's manuscript.

Arr. G. Weiser

(Dampen ⑤)

BIII

Killecrankie
(Planxty Davis)

The Connellan brothers, Thomas and William, were Irish harpers of the late 1600's. Thomas in particular wrote over 700 airs, but less than a dozen of their tunes have survived. "Killiecrankie" was written by Thomas when he was living in Scotland to commemorate the Battle of Killiecrankie which took place the 27th of July, 1689.

Thomas Connellan

Arr. G. Weiser

⑥ = D

♩ = **126** m.

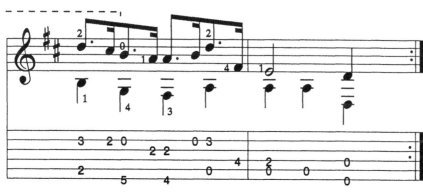

84

Kitty Tyrell

Anonymous

This anonymous tune is from the Bunting Collection, and is known to have been a favorite of the harpers who attended the Belfast gathering of 1792, when Bunting first began collecting Irish music.

Arr. G. Weiser

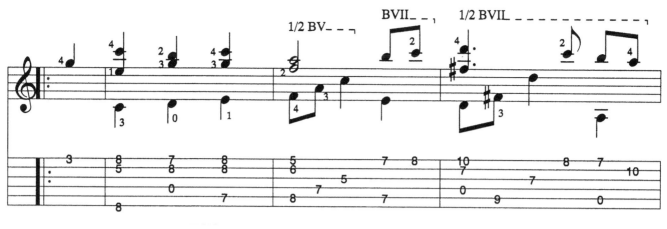

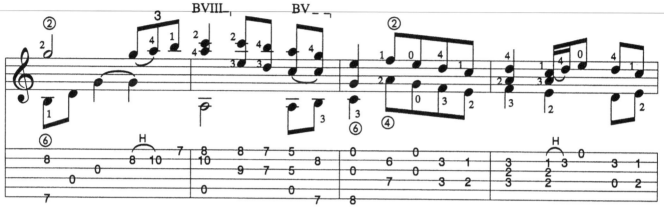

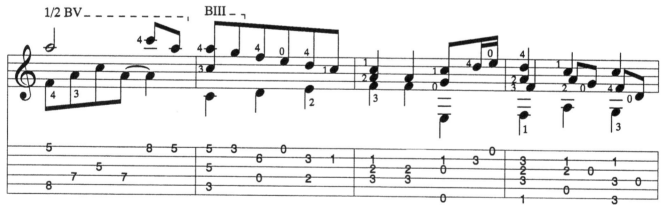

Lady Iveah

This tune is ascribed to either Thomas or William Connellan ~ Bunting lists both as being the composer in two different places in his work. The version here is from Bunting's printed version of the tune, which is more ornate than the manuscript version.

Lady Iveah was a noblewoman of County Down who live in the late seventeenth and early eighteenth centuries, and was widely known for her great personal charm.

Thomas Connellan

Arr. G. Weiser

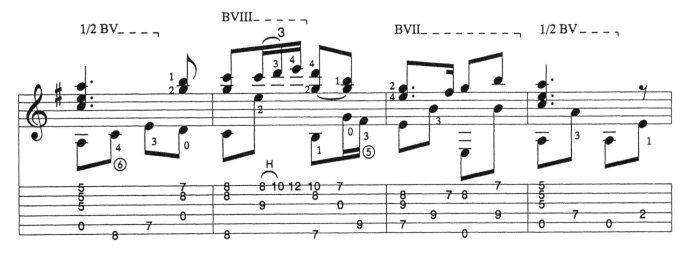

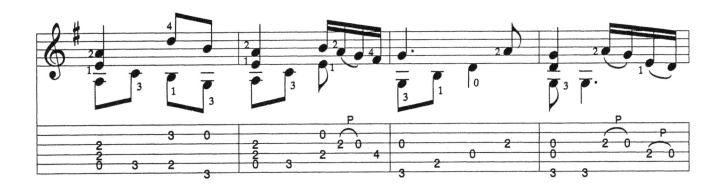

Limerick's Lamentation

This is a reworking of the Scottish tune "Lochaber No More" by the Irish harper Myles O'Reilly. The title refers to the capitulation of Limerick in 1691, when the Irish surrendered to the English forces after a long siege of the walled city. The ensuing period saw great hardship and oppression of the Irish by the English.

Myles O'Reilly

Arr. G. Weiser

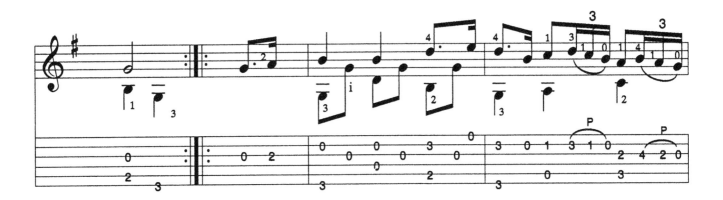

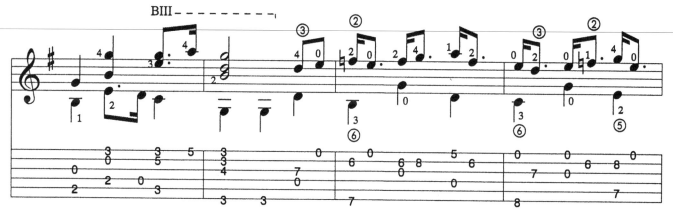

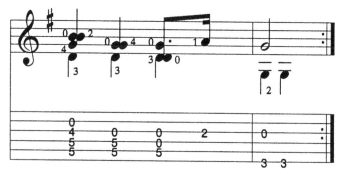

Simplified Melodies

"A" part, 2nd measure   "A" part, 6th measure and   "B" part, 2nd and 6th measures

"B" part, 14th measure

90

Love's A Tormenting Pain

It's hard to argue with the title! This lovely air is by William Connellan and was taken down by Bunting from Denis Hempson. Hempson, mentioned previously as the source of "Eileen Aroon," was the last of the traditional harpers. He played with long crooked nails in a style that was probably close to that of medieval harping, unlike his fellow contestants at the Belfast Convention, who played with the fleshy tips of the fingers and had repertories of more recent vintage.

Hempson's harp has survived and is known as the Downhill harp. One side of the sound chamber bears the following inscription, which tells us who made this instrument:

> *In the time of Noah I was green*
> *Since his flood I had not been seen*
> *Until seventeen hundred and two I was found*
> *By Cormac O'Kelly underground*
> *He raised me up to that degree*
> *Queen of Music you may call me*

William Connellan
Arr. G. Weiser

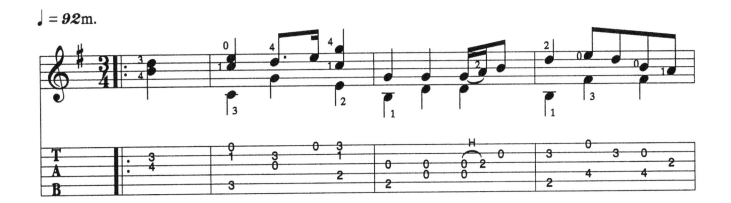

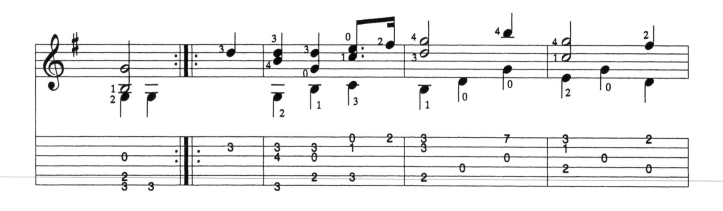

Miss Hamilton

This is the sole surviving original composition of Cornelius Lyons, (he also wrote variations to three tunes that are in the Bunting Collection ~ see "Eileen Aroon") and is doubly important as being the last known Irish harp tune to have been composed in the traditional manner. This arrangement is in the key of A rather than the original key of G and makes extensive use of three-part harmony.

Cornelius Lyons

Arr. G. Weiser

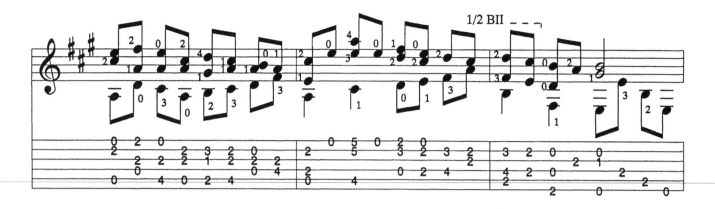

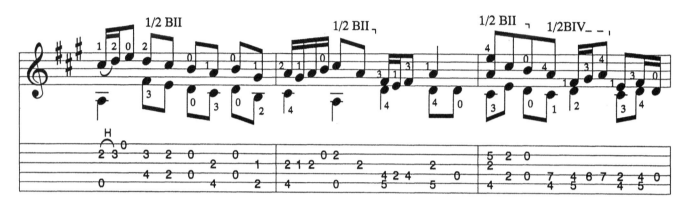

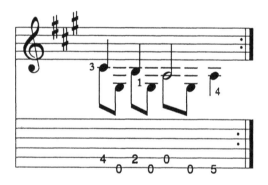

* Alternate Harmony ~ B part, measure 1

Molly McAlpin

Turlough O'Carolan said the same thing about this tune that Handel said of "Eileen Aroon"~ that he would rather have been the author of it than all his own compositions. Written by William Connellan, it was reworked by Carolan as "Carolan's Dream." This is the version given here.

Thomas Connellan

Arr. G. Weiser

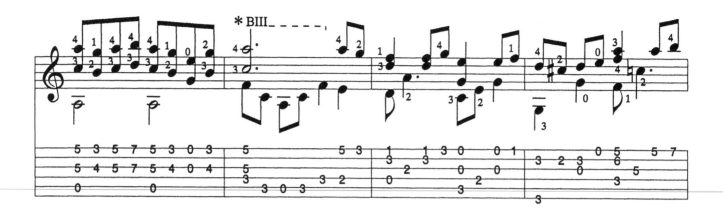

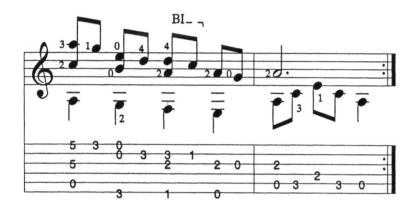

* Optional Harmony, "B" part, 4th measure

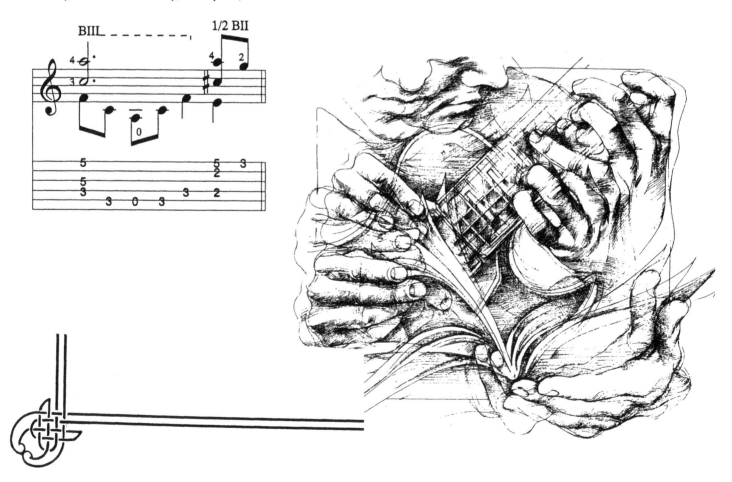

Molly St. George

This piece by Thomas Connellan can be found in the Bunting Collection and has been recorded by the Chieftans under the title of "The Tip of the Whistle". Because tinwhistle player Paddy Maloney couldn't recall the name of the tune or where he got it from, the liner notes to the second Chieftans' album simply say the name of the tune was "on the tip of his whistle".

Thomas Connellan

Arr. G. Weiser

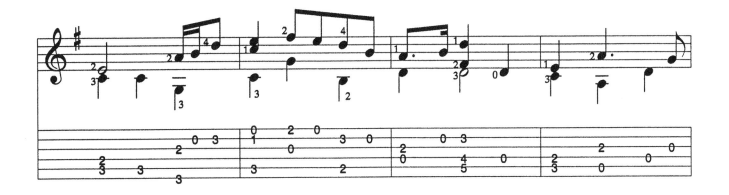

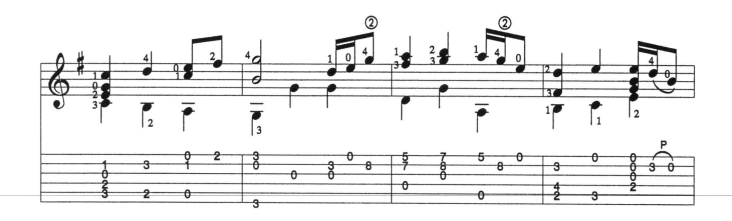

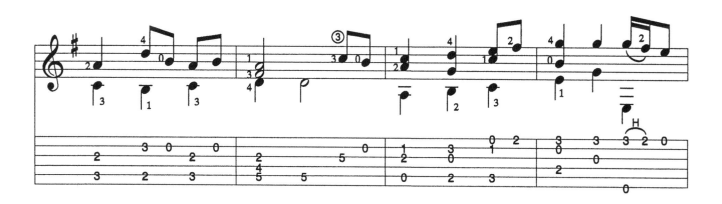

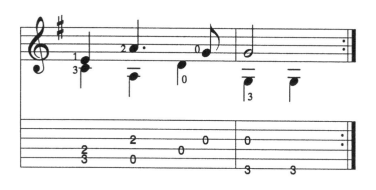

Port Atholl

Rory O'Cahan

This tune is ascribed to Rory Dhall O'Caithan and was composed in Scotland. It was later reworked by Turlough O'Carolan as "Katherine O'More," giving us a rare glimpse of the evolution of a Celtic harp tune over the years. "Port" is Gaelic for "tune," and Atholl is a place in Scotland whose Duke maintains the last private standing army in Europe (the troops wear sneakers rather than boots). This tune was probably composed for one of the Duke's predecessors.

Arr. G. Weiser

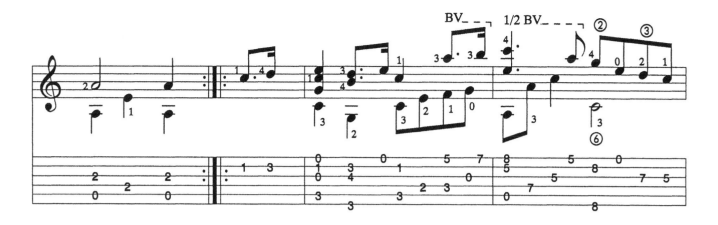

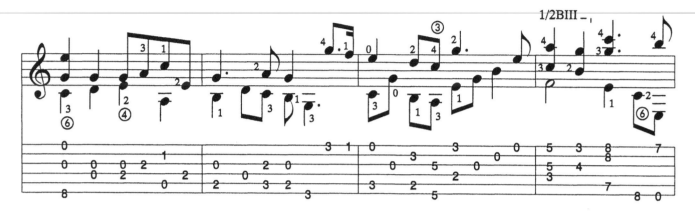

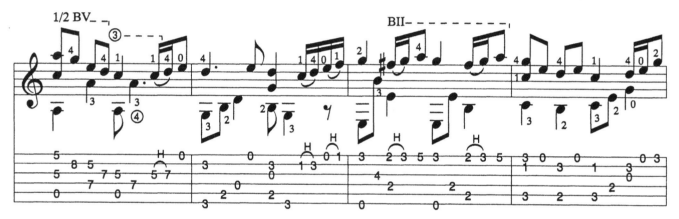

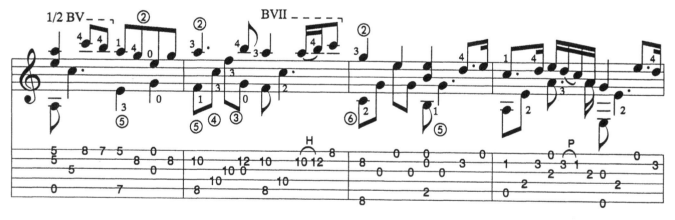

Alternate Fingering, B part, Measure 12

Port Lennox

Rory O'Cahan

This is another of Rory Dhall O'Caithan's tunes. This version of the tune comes from the playing
of Tony Jackson of the Scottish band *Ossian*. The second part of the tune is most beautiful ~
O'Caithan doubtless composed many other tunes of this quality which are now lost.

Arr. G. Weiser

⑥ = D

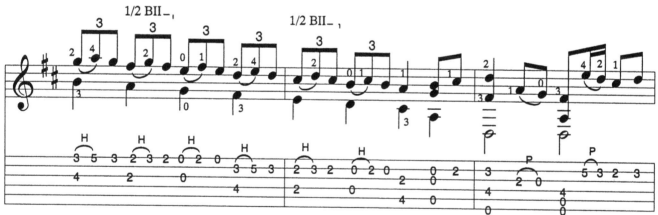

Port Patrick

Anonymous

This is a Scottish tune of unknown authorship. It consists of an air and a jig. Concluding a slow air with a jig (called a tailpiece) was a common practice during the seventeenth and eighteenth centuries; many of Carolan's pieces have such tailpieces.

Arr. G. Weiser

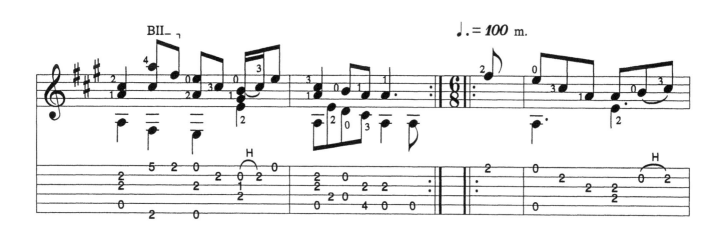

The Return From Fingal

According to tradition this was composed by Brian Boru's harper as a lament for his king's death at the battle of Clontarf. 'Fingal' in Gaelic means "territory of foreigners", in this case the Danes. The Chieftans recorded it on their fourth album as a part of the medley "The Battle of Aughrim".

Anonymous

Arr. G. Weiser

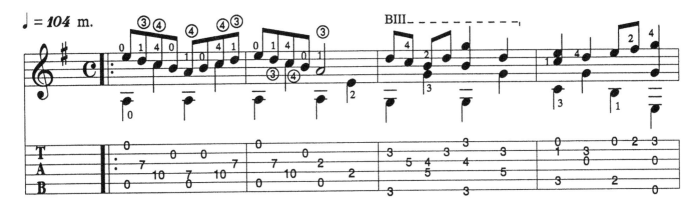

The Royal Lament

This tune was composed by a Scottish harper, John Garbh MacLean, upon the execution of Charles I in 1649. It consists of a stately air and a jig variation.

John Garbh MacLean

Arr. G. Weiser

variation ♩. = *80* m.

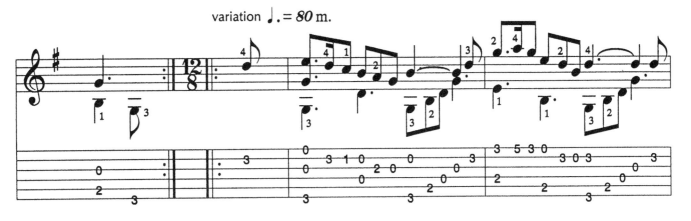

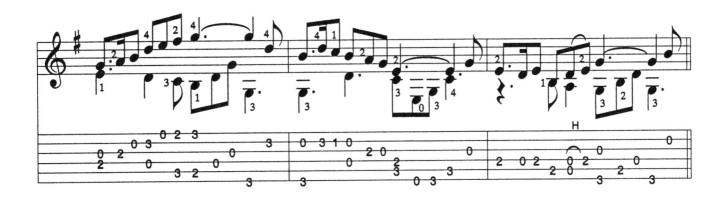

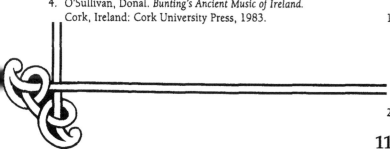

BIBLIOGRAPHY

1. Breathnach, Breandán. *Folk Music and Dances of Ireland.*
   Cork, Ireland: The Mercier Press, 1971.

2. Bunting, Edward. *The Ancient Music of Ireland.*
   Dublin, Ireland: Walton's Ltd., 1969.

3. Kinnaird, Alison. *The Harp Key.*
   Shillinghill Temple, Midlothian, Scotland: Kinmore Music, 1986.
   (Mrs. Kinnaird has also recently co-authored a book on the history of the
   Scottish harp, also published by Kinmore Music. Details were not available
   for this edition).

4. O'Sullivan, Donal. *Bunting's Ancient Music of Ireland.*
   Cork, Ireland: Cork University Press, 1983.

5. O'Sullivan, Donal. *Carolan ~ The Life, Times, and Music of an Irish Harper.*
   Louth, Lincolnshire, England: Celtic Music, 1983.
   (First Edition 1958 by Routledge Keegan Paul Ltd.)

6. Rimmer, Joan. *The Irish Harp.*
   Cork, Ireland: The Mercier Press, 1969.

7. Weiser, Glenn. *The Minstrel Boy - 85 Traditional Fiddle Tunes and Airs for
   Solo Guitar.*
   Port Chester, New York: Cherry Lane Music, 1989.

The following periodicals are recommended:

1. Acoustic Guitar
   P.O. Box 767
   San Anselmo, CA 74949
   (Articles about Carolan for
   the guitar can be found in #3
   and #20 of the magazine.)

2. The Folk Harp Journal
   P.O. Box 161
   Mt. Laguna, CA 92048

3. Sing Out!
   P.O. Box 5253
   Bethlehem, PA 18015

4. Fingerstyle Guitar
   7620 Delmonico Drive
   Colorado Springs, CO 80919

DISCOGRAPHY

Here is a list of Celtic recordings, most of which feature the harp. Where a recording contains tunes which appear in this book, the titles have been given after the entry. Unfortunately I have not been able to locate recorded sources for either "Kitty Tyrell" or "Love's a Tormenting Pain." ~ G.W.

1. Carolan's Receipt ~ Derek Bell. Shanachie 79013: Sheebeg and Sheemore, Carolan's Receipt, Lady Athenry, Fanny Poer, Mabel Kelly, Carolan's Quarrel with the Landlady, Carolan's Concerto, John O'Connor, Mrs. Maxwell, Carolan's Farewell to Music, Brighid Cruis (third and fourth airs).
2. Carolan's Favorite ~ Derek Bell. Shanachie 79020 ~ Hugh O'Donnell, Squire Woods' Lamentation, Lady St. John, Carolan's Welcome, Planxty O'Flinn, Katherine O'More, Dr. John Hart, Elizabeth MacDermott Roe, Michael O'Connor.
3. Derek Bell's Musical Ireland ~ Derek Bell. Shanachie 79042: Limericks' Lamentation, Eileen Aroon.
4. Chieftans 2. Shanachie 79022: George Brabazon (second air).
5. Chieftans 3. Shanachie 70933: Lord Inchinquin.
6. Chieftans 4. Claddagh CC14: Morgan Magan, Planxty Hewlett, The Return From Fingal, Molly St. George ("The Tip of the Whistle").
7. Chieftans 9. Columbia PC 36401: Madam Judge.
8. Planxty ~ same, Shanachie 79009: Planxty Irwin.
9. Jerry Holland ~ same. Rounder 7008: Planxty Browne.
10. Avenging and Bright ~ Charles Guard. Shanachie 79014: Brian Boru's March, Give Me Your Hand.
11. Heart Music ~ William Jackson. Iona 010: Port Lennox.
12. Ann's Harp ~ Ann Heyman. Clairseach 2381: Molly MacAlpin.
13. Let Erin Remember ~ Ann Heyman. Clairseach 8979.
14. The Harpers Land ~ Ann Heyman and Alison Kinnaird. Temple 013: Miss Hamilton, Lady Iveah.
15. The Harp Key ~ Alison Kinnaird. Temple 011: The Royal Lament, Killiecrankie, Port Atholl, Port Patrick.
16. The Harper's Gallery ~ Alison Kinnaird. Temple 003.
17. The Belfast Harp Festival ~ Grainne Yeats. Gael Linn 053/054: The Coolin.
18. Rennaisance of the Celtic Harp ~ Alan Stivell. Rounder 3067.
19. The New Strung Harp ~ Maire Ni Chathasaigh. Temple 019.
20. Legacy of the Scottish Harpers, Vols. I & II ~ Robin Williamson. Flying Fish 358, 390.
21. The Music of Turlough O'Carolan ~ Patrick Ball. Fortuna 1005.
22. O'Carolan's Dream ~ Patrick Ball. Fortuna 17061.
23. Secret Isles ~ Patrick Ball. Fortuna 17029.
24. Ancient Music for the Irish Harp ~ Derek Bell. Claddagh 59CD.
25. The Sweet Harp of My Land ~ Robin Huw Bowen. Flying Fish FF70610 (Welsh triple harp music).

The recordings listed above can be obtained from the following mail-order companies:

ANDY'S FRONT HALL
P.O. Box 307
Voorheesville, NY 12186
(518) 765-4193

ELDERLY INSTRUMENTS
P.O. Box 14210
Lansing, MI 48901
(517) 372-7890

ALCAZAR
P.O. Box 429
Waterbury, VT 05676
(800) 541-9904

More Great Guitar Books from Centerstream...

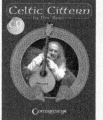

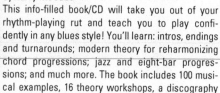

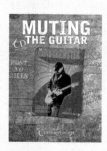